Ghosts of Glamorgan

Author: Karl-James Langford

Ghosts of Glamorgan

Part one of a series of books that discusses first-hand account stories from Glamorgan's ghostly past

Author:
Karl-James Langford MLitt

Illustrations (Excluding Pages 10, 11, 77 and 97)
Michelle Harrhy

Photography:
Michelle Harrhy
Mandie McCourt
Stephen Inkpen
Lynn Jones

Contributions:
Kelvin Dark
Anna Davies
Andrew Dexter
Michelle Harrhy
Stephen Inkpen
Desmond Johnson
Brian Jones
Mandie McCourt

Proof Reader:
William Howells

Karl-James Langford
Copyright 2019 ©

First Edition (Impression 1)
Published by **Archaeology Cymru Media**
Publisher No. 698848
ISBN: 978 0952939450
Retail Price: **£11.99**

Printed by:
Integrated Graphics Ltd
Units 8 and 9
Palmerston Workshops
Barry
CF63 2YZ

Author can be contacted directly on:
karljlangford@hotmail.com
or Tel: 07437 747402

INSPIRED AND DEDICATED
TO THE MEMORY OF **DESMOND JOHNSON**

"There were a few stories
to talk about"

Karl-James Langford MLitt

Dedicated to Phyllis Langford
who passed away this year.

With the crushing loss of
someone so important in my life,
I just wanted her to be proud of me!

*"Moving about the landscape,
these little gems can be discoveries
that assist our understanding
of our past, through ghosts."*

Karl-James Langford MLitt

Preface and Introduction

This book is an account of some real ghost stories from South Wales. Very few of these stories have ever seen any public audience, or even moved away from the conversations of a small group of friends. Further editions may create a series of books, that will be available for publication in the future examining many more ghost stories across Wales.

Stephen Inkpen was the first to offer to assist me; he took up the gauntlet to provide us with two belters in this publication; the first being The Lady of the Rock. As with most stories, this is a tragic story, one of unrequited love, with more questions than answers. It is a story of a stubborn Banog girl, that chooses to marry anyone she wishes too. The boy she wants to marry goes to sea, only to marry the Banog girl in her dad's eyes if he comes home after making his fortune. With her horse, the Banog girl heads into the mountain every evening to look out for the boy's homecoming. I think readers can guess what happened. For Stephens other stories, it is a little darker, so read on.

It is with sadness that Desmond Johnson born in 1927 who contributed four great stories for this book, has now left us in 2018, but he lives on in his work. I am very grateful for the help of his daughter Lynn who has been invaluable in clarifying the stories for this book. Desmond's stories are based around the period after the First World War and running beyond the Second World War. We hear about 'just these feet', coming up the stairs, they were naily boots (hobnail) you could tell because they were heavy sounding at Woodford House. Then we get out of the way, quickly, and jump into the hedge, and when we looked, there was no sign of ghostly horses at all. A further Desmond story is the short story of the Tramp of Llanmaes, but when he got into the pub, and on enquiring about him, the tramp was dead. And what lead to me even thinking about producing this book? 'The Littleman', thanks to Desmond. On another note, there is a Youtube video on his stories, that we made together before his passing.

It was that very Youtube video that brought our attention to Andrew Dexter; he wanted so much for his stories of the Bargoed Gladstone Villa be made more public. And as houses go, this is a frightening one. I prefer a night at the haunted Skirid inn than this place.

On delivering leaflets one day around Wick in the Vale of Glamorgan, I came across Kelvin Dark, who wrote down the story of the man of Stoney Lane. I loved it so much and felt the story had to be offered to print. Chatting to me in a similar way to one of Archaeology Cymru valley students, a confident Brian Jones got me to record ghostly stories from the Rhondda Valleys from a place called Trealaw.

Then we turn to Anna Davies. A very recent sighting, but a ghost that may be close to 900 years old. As Anna stares, she tells us, "he never turned around to look at me!" Who was this figure? The bottom half of the man covered in the cloak, an ancient style garment. An apparition that is very straight forward and simple. She tells us, that, "I've seen him only once, and no sound from him either." Read Anna's story.

Mandie McCourt, a regular on the Archaeology Cymru ghost, walks takes us to examine four short but exciting sightings. The girl at the stile, she is just seen there and nowhere else. The man on a bike that we have seen him come down the hill straight to the barn alongside the old road, what is that all supposed to mean? And we couldn't forget to mention the ghosts at two separate churches in the Vale of Glamorgan.

Last but not least, in this publication are my own direct experience of this ghostly landscape. But as for sightings and activities, one place in South Wales has a truly dark side, full of those things that go bump in the night. The route through Blaen-y-Cwm that takes you to the sea is undoubtedly dripping in horror. And then there is Merthyr Mawr that continues to be a hot spot of activity for my regular ghostly walks.

Did I ever believe in real ghosts? The answer is probably no, before meeting Michelle Harrhy in 2015. We even have a first-hand account from Michelle also. But since then, the ghost walks have totally changed my angle, and there is the usual statement from Michelle, "don't bring them home with you!" Indeed, direct experiences have changed things for me. What do I mean, well read this book!

All stories have been placed into a category as follows for 'feelings', actual recent first-hand account as 'sightings' or oral lead 'stories', there are several that have a mixed element to them: sightings, feelings and stories.

Resolven

Fe

Maesteg

Swansea

Merthyr Mawr

Bridgend

Dunraven

Corntown

Pen

Llanmae

Monknash

Marcross

Llantwit
Major

Brecon

are

Bargoed

Ystrad
Mynach

banog

Pontypridd

Caerphilly

Newport

nharan

ridge

Cardiff

Llantrithyd

Penarth

Gileston

Barry

CONTENTS

GHOSTLY HORSES OF LLANMAES

DESMOND JOHNSON

This story from Desmond Johnson takes us to the northwestern outskirts of Llanmaes, near Llantwit Major, Vale of Glamorgan to the Old Rectory (was a functioning rectory until 1988, until the church sold it into private hands). The landscape has changed very little in the 80 odd years that this story originated. In interviewing Desmond about this little gem I was aware of the Frampton ghost horse associated with Adam de Frankton, but I felt that the link was tenuous, because of the number of horses mentioned according to Desmond, "definitely more than one there was".

So lets therefore begin. We were in Llanmaes by the back of the rectory; it was a windy dark night, and we were ferreting ... poaching, it was a long time ago! We could hear horses galloping in a field, so we jumped into the hedge and got out the way. But we didn't see any horses at all pass us. So I said about it weeks after to this chap I talked too. I asked him "has the farmer got any horses?" and he replied, "that the farmer hasn't got any horses in the field". "Well, he did that night!" I remarked jokingly.

There was more than one horse, quite a few by the sounds of it we felt at the time. I think it was the cavalry. You could hear them coming, the horses like that would be heard galloping towards you a mile away. It was quick as that we just heard them galloped past. When we looked, we were hoping to see them, and we didn't sadly.

THE CAT AT DUNRAVEN CASTLE

MICHELLE HARRHY

I was sitting with Karl-James talking on the steps to the east outside of this ruined house known as Dunraven castle, Southerndown, Vale of Glamorgan heading into the now disused car-park in front of the woods. Then suddenly a black cat runs in front of me, and he just disappeared. I said to Karl-James, "did you see that cat", and he said, "no". I followed the cat with my eyes. It wasn't massive, it was a black cat, like Merlin. I have a cat that has been with me for nearly ten years called Merlin.

I didn't notice its eyes; this cat went running too quick in front of me. I didn't see a colour or anything; it was a black cat. It was in the dusk time, clear night, moonlight night, headed towards the direction in front of me across to where the gardens are. The stone enclosed gardens of the old house still exist.

There is a row of dogs graves within the garden that remained after the demolition of the Dunraven House in 1963. Maybe this cat was heading towards the place of the tombs, to where cats may also have been interred. However, it is presumed they were all graves of dogs... maybe one, just one is the actual grave of our cat from this story.

THE BLACK SHUCK AT THE MERTHYR MAWR BEECH TREES

Karl-James Langford

While on a Ghost Experience walk for Archaeology Cymru in the early days, I lead the party back from the site of the New Inn, Merthyr Mawr (South West of Bridgend), it was getting a little dusky. It had been an enthusiastic walk, and 2016 by far was the best of times for these activities for us. We were nearly at the Beech trees towards the northeast of the village of Merthyr Mawr; after heading off the 'dangerous' footpath from the New Inn. I headed to a point halfway along the avenue, these trees remember the events of the New Inn, these trees are close on 300 years old, and directly along the route from the New Inn; now alas partly a footpath.

I suffer from Obsessive Compulsive Disorder (OCD), so I sent my partner Michelle Harrhy forward to lead the group, towards one of my final ghost story stopping places. I was at the back to gather my thoughts, and to retrace my steps (if you have OCD you'll understand what I mean, in short, I was making sure I hadn't dropped anything or moreover left anyone behind). For some reason, the light seemed to be fading fast, I felt very uneasy, and this time, there was something left behind. My inner self was saying to me, "that I was to look behind me", as I was focusing on getting to the group.

The answer was a big resounding, "yes to look behind me", there was something left to 'check', but this was following me. I hadn't ritually closed the space we had been too, to stop the spirits following me. Ritually closing space is something I perform to prevent benevolent and evil spirits coming home with me, as they had done before. The group was at least 50 metres in front of me, along the avenue of Beech trees.

I stopped, felt something behind me, was it one of the group, "don't be silly", I thought. It was now dusky and darkening rapidly; the group seemed much further away than a few metres. It wasn't cold, far from it, a comfortable, un- comfortableness- if that makes sense. I turned towards the direction of the path from the New Inn, swerved my whole body around to the right, "why do that, you'll only need to check it a little again, retrace a few steps, there was a reason, look on the right", those were my thoughts. "The wall on the right. Look into the darkening gloom" I exclaimed to myself. "There, there it is... an aberration heading into the Beech tree's now on the left. It's black, not that big, not a shuck, but four legs, and is it coming at me, a dog of some-kind. Nobody is around at that moment, and I could be in the darkest forest for all I knew. It slowly moves across the road, on a mission. I don't understand what is happening; it came from the face of the wall on the right, I moreover don't understand what is happening because it is a ghost, right?"

I had told people about shucks before; and black dogs, big wild dogs etc.., but didn't or wouldn't believe it, now there is the evidence. Now I start to freak out inside, "this is real", as the creature disappears onto the other side of the road, I scream out, and begin to 'bloody' run towards the group. "I have just seen a black dog", I'm shouting. The group then stop; they are all in a row, and turn around and look towards me.

This black dog is no-longer behind me now, any ghost would be frightened off by this nutty man dressed in a Dickensian outfit with a top hat on. From that moment onwards with this evidence, I was convinced, "Ghosts do in-fact exist". The group looked and looked, one or two imagined there were things there, but no black animal was anywhere to be seen.

Since then we have been back to have an all-night vigil, other New Inn walks have occurred, but for want of reason for over a year, we hadn't been back. And then two walks in a row in 2018, not just me but everyone on those walks saw a ghost, and more sightings and feelings in that lane, overall the sense of place the focus of activity and the evil at the avenue of the Beech tree's, and not a place of good things. More of this in the second book.

THE LITTLE MAN DOWN THE LEYS

DESMOND JOHNSON

This sighting takes us to a time before the summer, before the Power Station, Aberthaw, Vale of Glamorgan was there just after the Second World War.

The tide was coming in, and I was down there duck shooting, and I sat on the bank like I'm sitting now (sat back upright as on a chair) and the dog in front of me. And as there was a beautiful night, moonlit night, and patch; that's the dog's name, he started to growl looking over my shoulder, and he was growling. And I looked around, and there was this little fella standing there with a peaked cap, and a waste coat done up, and his trousers tied up like that (trousers folded and tied on knee); 'know' the old fashioned way to stop the rats going up. I think I turned around and said, "where did you come from?" He just disappeared, but he was as plain as looking at Lynn now (Lynn Johnson, Desmond's daughter).

And I have seen him, after that, since the power station has been there. I was down there one night, same sort of night, beautiful moonlit night, white cloud, mackerel cloud, and he was walking on the sea wall. I went up on the sea wall and walked after him, and I couldn't gain on him, you know it was the same distance all the time, as fast as I went it didn't alter the distance.

The first night that I saw him again was like it was when the river was forming an oxbow a couple of acres of ground. And I was sat under the bank, and I thought it was a friend of mine; Laurie Hopkins from St. Athan. And he walked, he went through the sheep, and they didn't move, they were lying down, the sheep didn't move. So I thought, "go and have a look, cause there were always ducks on the bend in the river". I got to the bend in the river, and there were just no marks in the mud. No marks in the mud I called Laurie and no answer, but there was no one there, no marks in the mud or anything. And This person who went that way didn't come back, he just disappeared.

"Well I've seen him, that's three times".

But I've known two other people that had seen him; once when the sand dunes were there, before the golf course, there were sand dunes there. And there was Tommy Liscum, there was a pub there, the Ocean building or Ocean pub or something, and he was with his wife to be in the sand dunes, lying in the sand dunes. And she said to him," Tommy" she said, "there is a little man watching us", and he turned around and started to shout at him and he disappeared. And he described him to me as exactly the same; waistcoat jacket, peak cap and his trousers. The waistcoat was brown, trousers brown, all it was matching, they were brown, he could see the buttons and everything as clear as day.

And then there was another person a shift foreman (Stan Lavery from Barry) on nights with me on the cement works, Rhoose cement works. He was down there one night he said, "fishing", and I said, "go on then carry on", and he said, "I happened to look, and there was a little man standing alongside me", and I said, "what was he dressed like", and he had described him exactly the same way, I just said,

"I couldn't make it out there is no answer to, is it, is there?"

Because he just disappears, when I spoke to him, I'm talking to myself. But the dog could see him as well, 'see', but the sheep couldn't. Or the sheep didn't see him. You couldn't see any leg movement. There was no sort of stepping, he just glided along, and I went after him on the sea wall, to see if I could catch up with him. But if he was real or not, and when we got underneath the end of the wall under the caravans at Fontygary (between Aberthaw and Rhoose, Vale of Glamorgan), there was no one there, not a soul.

"A great story that spurred me on to write this book."

THE LADY OF THE ROCK

STEPHEN INKPEN

This story was told to me by my grandparents Avis (born in 1913) & Frederick Williams (born in 1910). My Nan was born in Trebanog (a village South of Pontypridd at the foot of the Rhondda Valleys) and lived there all her life. Her father, Mr.F.W.Brock came to Trebanog and built most of the houses in the original village (Trebanog Road, Brocks Terrace & Dan-y-graig Terrace), he was friends with the old farming families from here and also heard the stories from them. It's a well-known story in Trebanog.

Once, long ago, there was a wealthy farmer who lived at Rhiwgarn Fawr Farm in Trebanog. The farmer and his wife had no sons and only one daughter, so the farmer decided to find a suitable respectable husband for his daughter. Being a Banog girl, the daughter did not take kindly to this news, and informed her father that he was too late, for she had already fallen in love and knew all too well who she was going to marry! The farmer demanded to know who it was that had stolen his daughter's heart. Well as it turned out she had fallen for a farm labourer from one of the small cottages on the other side

The path leading up the mountain from Rhiwgarn Farm.
Taken by Stephen Inkpen

of the hill, this was not acceptable to the farmer, and off he went to talk it out with the boy, leaving his daughter in tears.

View across the field, looking up the Rhondda Fach, near to where the 'Lady of the Rock' fell. Taken by Stephen Inkpen

The two men talked well into the night, and the old farmer began to like the boy as he was much more intelligent than he had realized. Despite this, the boy had no wealth, no land and no experience in running a farm! In the early hours, it was decided that the boy would leave Trebanog and go off to make his fortune at sea, but he would soon return and marry the girl he loved!

That morning the two lovers said farewell, and the farmer's daughter promised that she would ride up onto the mountain every evening to look down at sea and watch for his return.

Months passed by, and every evening, she would ride up the mountain as she promised, and each evening, her heart grew heavier as no word came from her love. One evening in the early autumn, she sat looking at the ships on the distant sea and tears flowed down her cheeks. She watched for too long, and before she realized it, it had begun to get dark, she wiped her eyes and turned the horse to home. She had not gone far when a thick fog came down on the mountain, and in the growing darkness, she became disorientated and soon lost her way. In increasing darkness and more impenetrable fog, her panic grew, and her horse became jittery. The horse slipped on the way down the path and began to become stressed, in its fear the horse jumped over the rocks into the fog taking itself over a cliff, and they both fell to their deaths.

The lady is still seen from time to time as she wanders the mountain, waiting for her lover to return home. No one knows if he ever did return. The horse can be heard on foggy nights as it clip-clops home along the track to Rhiwgarn farm.

WOODFORD ON THE BEACH ROAD

DESMOND JOHNSON

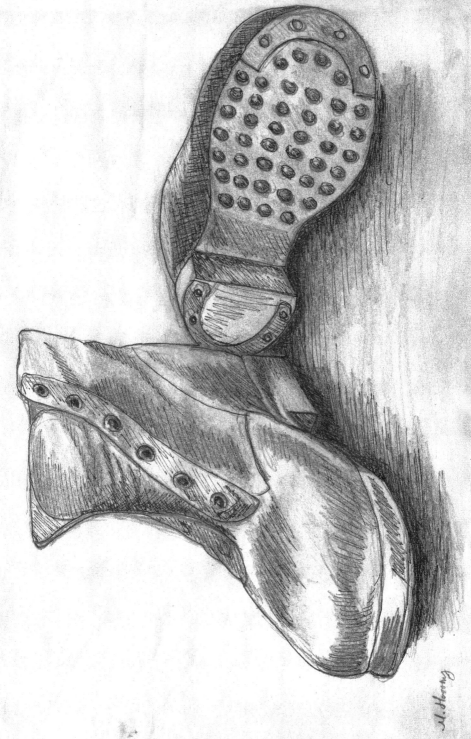

Having been a very adventurous lad, Desmond Johnson found himself in some exotic locations. Woodford house was no exception. Woodford House is located on a stretch of road fondly known as The Beach Road; its actual name for reference is, in fact, Colhugh Street, Llantwit Major, Vale of Glamorgan heading towards the coast at Colhugh Bay and the Iron Age Bank and Ditched enclosure.

Like many locations up and down the coastline throughout the First and Second World Wars, our large mansions and residential buildings were utilized as housing by servicemen and women of all nations. Woodford was to serve as quarters for troops serving in the First World War, unlike many others that accommodated them: Candleston Merthyr Mawr, Ham Manor Llantwit Major and Dunraven Southerndown, it would survive into the modern day. You could imagine that the wear and tear in use over wartime, would have taken its toll on these once proud buildings.

This story takes us to a point in time around the late 1930s just before the outbreak of the Second World War. And when you read the term Naily boots, think of heavy black hobnail boots.

Between the wars, Woodford House on the beach road; the old rectory, it had been lain empty. There had been soldiers in it during the war (World War I 1914-1918), and they'd gone. Russel my cousin and I went in nosing around Woodford House, as all adventurous lads would do, we headed upwards. After negotiating the bare wooden stairs we found ourselves on the first floor, there were just wooden floors. Preoccupied with exploring, we became startled while we were up there, by an ominous sound. We could hear boots clumping, 'naily boots' coming up the stairs!

We quickly fled from the landing. We found ourselves wondering whether to go into a room, the second bedroom along on the passage. But continued running, was there anyone pursuing us? The landing continued to go right around the back of that house, and there are doors in the wall where you can go into the attic. So we didn't know who it was coming in, so got up into the gods. We were squinting; peeping in through the doors and the sound went into the bedroom below us. The sound of the naily boots was walking, towards the window, but we could see there was no one there. How could this be, were we hearing things, both of us at the same time, this did not seem right.

Just the noise was enough to chill us to the bone. We got out of there a bit quick; there was no sign of anybody.

A NORMAN KNIGHT AT PENLLYN

ANNA DAVIES

I live about a quarter of a mile from an old medieval building/house that has been extended onto extensively over the years; particularly in the mid-1800s into a family home. The house is within the Parish of Penllyn which is not far from the A48 and Pentre Meyrick, Vale of Glamorgan (West of Cowbridge).

The time of year was early autumn, the temperature wasn't cold or windy, the weather, it was reasonably warm, fine evening and the sun was shining, and the time of day was 4 pm. I was walking up the path towards the medieval house. A little while before [days] I remembered a large branch from a Beech tree that had come down across the track, it was laying horizontal, but the side branches were vertical.

It was in broad daylight that I suddenly stopped with shock, because there in front of me by the fallen Beech branch was a Norman man with a plain face. Was this man in a pre-skirmish thought! He was wearing a very long dull plain woollen moss green cloak, and with one of the traditional Norman metal helmets. The helmet was that traditional long shape dome with the nasal piece protection bar on it.

He wasn't looking directly at me but slightly off to the left. He didn't at all turn his body, or face to face me. A Norman man, a soldier, but wasn't totally dressed as one, the gown covering his Armour. He looked completely lost in thought, "thinking it would be, that he was wondering what on earth he should do".

The colour of the only visible piece of clothing was a significant detail, the woollen cloak went all the way down to ground level. I couldn't see hands or arms, the body shape was completely contained by the cloak.

And I stood, first of all, my heart was pounding, and obviously I didn't want to carry on walking past him, if I had, I would have been within two feet of him. And I must have stood there for 4 to 5 minutes wondering, "what I should do and what on earth was going to happen". I was feeling perturbed while I was there because I was there long enough, and looking at him long enough to know, that I wasn't imagining anything and it wasn't a trick of the light or a branch. Or anything like that, it was a real person.

"How did I feel? This I thought wasn't a 'simple' occurrence, whilst I was standing there, I asked myself, 'am I seeing this?'

I kept thinking, 'am I seeing this?' I was questioning myself. I didn't want to go nearer, further forward, as there was no doubt there was someone there. I was there long enough to really affirm that it wasn't a trick of the light. No less than 30ft away".

There was no movement from him, from his head or anything else. And I just stood still stupidly there looking at him, and I had no camera and could take no photographs. After 4 to 5 minutes, I sort of turned around and started to walk down the path. After a few steps, I turned my head around to look at him, and he was no longer there. But the visibility was perfect and there is no doubt it was a man, and I was actually looking at someone, a three-dimensional person.

I've been up to that path many many times, not just in daylight, but in darkness with a torch and in the moonlight. Having walked that path a few times, I haven't seen anything like that before or since.

This story will leave with the question was the 'Norman man' a lord of the manor, a warrior or someone else? We may never know.

Sometimes I ask the question of those who give me these stories, "did they originate from the village?" If so the story may be indicative of that part of us passed down through the persons DNA, a real event, an echo of an actual event. I asked Anna where she felt her family originated from. She replied,

"I originated from Llantwit Major, but I have no historical links with Penllyn. My mother was from London and my father from Newcastle."

So as an author I cannot forward any explanation for this sighting.

THE CHILDREN OF BLAEN-Y-CWM

KARL-JAMES LANGFORD

The landscape of the Cistercian grange of Monknash has a small number of ghost stories associated with it, including the one about 'Sion Celwydd'. The landscape heads from the Plough and Harrow pub, Monknash to the coast known as Cwm Nash, West of Llantwit Major, Vale of Glamorgan. But from the Plough and Harrow at Monknash, the landscape has a genuinely evil tone about it. It should 'be noted' that many a landlord at the Plough and Harrow has to say the least become a little unhinged by their residency there.

What is lacking from the interwoven history of Monknash is a written down 'chapter' of ghost stories about the Valley of Blaen-y-Cwm, we aim to address that here. Blaen-y-Cwm is the stretch of public footpath that continues from the open public road, and that leads towards a dead end in the form of the actual coastline. This stretch is also known as Burial Lane. At the top of this juncture, there is also a private road that leads slightly west towards a house. The Cwm until you are upon it, is almost mythical, a hidden gorge in a matter of words, and it plays well into the storytelling of Cymry tradition with the likes of Merlin and his kin.

Blaen-y-Cwm can be experienced as three sections, and genuinely frightening are upper and middle. The Upper part contains the mill leat, the mill, and at times a rocky pathway flanked on the left (east) by quarrying and a steep drop towards the Nash brook on the right (west). The middle section that we shall fondly in daylight that is, refer too as the 'shaded glade', at night however it is unerringly frightening. This very section can be muddy in winter, and a canopy of branches and leaves protects you from the suns rays, and then raindrops in a storm. And finally the windswept third section in the open, with the distinct sound of the sea, and its salty aroma, it seems fairly more friendly on this stretch.

After 30 or so guided walks on behalf of Ghost Experience Cymru (part of Archaeology Cymru) through the Blaen-y-Cwm, mainly in the dark, I feel that I am now experienced enough to sense a presence down there. And what have I sensed? But before we discuss the whys and wherefore all, take my advice, I would not recommend heading down there at dusk by oneself. Don't go down there without a torch.

The whole story of the ghosts at Blaen-y-Cwm is a long-winded background that I offer here — reported to the national media in March 2014, were the monks' bones. These monks bones that belonged to a cemetery were a national sensation. The grave of this unfortunate monk was meant to be excavated by the Glamorgan-Gwent Archaeological Trust as they claimed on a BBC news item. Well over a year and a half later, they still had failed to do the excavation, even though they had been paid the funding from the state to excavate the mortal remains, the corrupt world that is Welsh Archaeology. The bones still in place and entirely on view, 'against the dignity of the poor buried soul' (all thanks to the poor archaeological practice of the Glamorgan-Gwent Archaeological Trust) were to be part of the locations to visit, of my first ever historical and Ghost Experience Cymru walk series for Archaeology Cymru.

The day before that momentous Friday they had been still in place, that is 'dem bones'. The walk had taken place in relatively clement weather, although there had been the odd torrent of rain, just as we reached the coast. The first part of the walk was over, the historical stories, now as the light had failed was the turn of the ghosts. As we reached the monk's bones, and with total horror, someone had maliciously smashed them out of the rock with stones, with the broken fragments laying on the beach below. This heinous act marked what was install for us as we walked back.

The ghosts that evening and over several further evenings haunted the Monknash walks. We started to drop the history content, and occupy on the ghostly sightings and feelings we had been described by others, and lots of my own.

Back to the very first walk, I made a small survey of what people had felt and seen, in particular along the Blaen-y-Cwm stretch, two individuals came forward, with chillingly the same story, and neither of them was linked. The steward; a dear friend of mine Tom Savery of Barry, that night recanted that he felt he had become followed by a presence along the shaded glade section of the Cwm towards the coast, and then another true sceptic on the walk, recited the very same story the steward had offered. For a time, what they had described seemed as if it was a real person. The entity followed them back out again.

"How could this be?"

They would have had to pass a real person, for it to have turned up behind them. Therefore, the conclusion has to be that this was a ghostly entity; attached to the group

But as the walk at Monknash took on a once a month occurrence for the first couple of years, the stories grew. It was usually women who told these stories, one remarked, "I could not bear to walk on the right-hand side (west) of Blaen-y-Cwm" after passing the mill towards the shaded valley. Then there were the tell-tale sounds of somebody walking on the opposite side of the Cwm just before you reach the 'shaded glade'. What is more critical about these spectra sounds, is that more than one individual was convinced it was shuffling and stomping around, thoughts that it could be a 10-year-old boy, came to the minds of many!

Actually, within the shaded glade well before it culminates before the footpath to head into the last section (third section, towards the sea), I used to tell the story of the Gwrach-y-rhibyn. A frightful hag that haunted the villages around the coast eyeing up her next victim for 'Mr. Death'. This location is where activity was at it's most potent, with variously shaped orbs and sounds crackling in the bushes all around. We took the time to write down some of these first-hand accounts taken over four years.

"As soon as the story of the Gwrach was being recanted in the Blaen-y-Cwm Burial Lane, there was like shuffled footsteps towards the side of the path, and then it was just as if somebody was walking about. I told Michelle who was beside me, and then it just moved from the tree into the undergrowth or the side of me, and it was just like a weird noise. It was as if somebody was there and I flashed the torch, and nobody was present, there was no reflection of animal eyes or nothing, there was nothing there."

It was almost as if the real story of the Gwrach would conjure up mischief. Some stories would attract positive or negative energy. A further account states:

"Saw red lights before you mentioned the witch."
Monknash was the very walk in 2015 that I was a total sceptic in the

belief of ghosts. As activity increased on this walk and the others, a year of such trails and I was to be a true believer. And such was the belief in me by those attending the walks; I started to channel this occurrence. Based on this, we present this account:

"As we entered the woods (...shaded glade...) the atmosphere changed, I felt there was something evil there, and that's why I said to Karl don't go any further down the path; whatever it was, wanted to scare us and maybe hurt one of us, but between Karl and I, we held them back."

And then there was this:

"I also felt the presence of a little girl, but I think she is connected to Karl."

It started to become clear that I had some connection with these entities, whether they were innocuous or malign.

And then there was one area of the Cwm that we have missed out of this story. The mill started to become more and more active, with the once-monthly visits. By the following year, we would run walks for different age groups. The path above the mill would have a different effect on children than it would for adults. Some children remarked the sentiments of one child:

"At first, at the Blaen-y-Cwm mill, I felt a small figure pass through me, and it sent a shiver down my spine."

We would never go actually down the slope to the mill alongside the river, health and safety implications made that impossible, but never the less, the flow of activity was powerful. One middle-aged woman reported.

"I felt something push me and almost fell over."

The children in the woods were the overall theme of activity there. And it is with no wonder why children should be the over ridding case for Blaen-y-Cwm, due to the proximity with the mill. Children have been known to play within the mill leats (Llandaf Cardiff has such a story). And as sluices are released, the race would take children to the mill head. The children then shot out onto the 'overshot' water wheel, and were turned onto the treads of the mill wheel and then drowned.

On a final note, and I'm sure in a future book in this series we can discuss them more, the monks. Come to think of it, the monks here; before the dissolution of the monasteries in the late 1530s, can only be described as not being the best-spirited individuals, they were brigands of the highest calibre.

The monks had actively wrecked ships; after all,

Blaen-y-Cwm by Michelle Harrhy

it was their stretch of coast, and only they could have sanctioned the murder of those wrecked out at sea. The monks would drag 'token bodies' along Burial Lane to keep up the pretence that they were godly, and prepare the bodies for burial, after sounding cynical "the terrible loss of life at sea". These individuals had already been stripped of the worldly goods at the coastline, by the same monks that were now performing their final rights. These Cistercian monks are to be seen to be of a total abhorrent nature, malign and evil to the worst degree, and for one I agree with the Dissolution of the Monasteries under King Henry VIII.

THE GHOST OF STONEY LANE

KELVIN DARK

Back in 1978, my girlfriend and I were driving home after a night out; the time was about 11.40pm and around May time. We had just driven through the village of Corntown, South of Bridgend and turned left into Stoney Lane; this is a short cut up to the back lane to Wick.

In those days there were no houses on the left side of the lane as you drive up, only about four or five on the right side and then the lane turns sharp right about halfway up.

As we were driving, a man walked out from the field on the left side of the road about thirty yards in front of us; he did not look at the car, he was in the full view of the headlights. We were travelling at about twenty-five miles an hour. The odd thing was, he had a large sack over his right shoulder, and the bottom of his trousers was tied up like the old farm workers used to.

He walked straight across the road into the garden of the house on the right; there was no colour to him. He was like a dark shadow, but with shape definition, we could see him plain enough, he never at anytime looked or took any notice of the car. As he went into the garden we came to where we would be of level with him, all the windows were lit up, but there was no sign of him.

The next day I went back to the lane as I knew something was just not right about all this, on the left-hand side of the lane there was an earth stone bank or sometimes called a hedge. Then about five feet high and in it was a farm gateway into a field, the old wooden gate was rotten, hanging off its hinge. And the gateway into a field, the old wooden gate was rotten, and the gateway covered in a thick bramble bush and also most of the lane on that side. There was no way that anyone had walked through the gate, for a very long time! And that is where he came from; there is no doubt in my mind about that.

Thirty plus years later, I was having a pint in the Five Bells public house in Bridgend and was telling the story to a friend of mine, who was brought up in the village and lives at the bottom of Stoney Lane. On hearing what I had told him, he said: "Kelvin, lots of people have seen him, so you did see what you thought you had". He said, "he was a great uncle of his and a bit of a poacher and a black marketer in the war, and came from St. Athan".

So there you have it, our story of when we saw the ghost of Stoney Lane! Houses have been built all the way up to the bend in the lane now, and the old gate and earth stone bank, long gone! But I have often thought that he must still walk his track some nights searching for loot, and carrying his sack of the perhaps poached game, but I have never been back to look!

MAN ON A BIKE

MANDIE McCOURT

Ghosts suddenly becoming lost from view, is very much what this short story of a man on a bike tells us.

There is a ghost of an old man on a push bike that rides down the hill from Wick, and then past the Horseshoes, Marcross, Vale of Glamorgan (West of Llantwit Major) and disappears into the barn opposite. Now I was told by my dad (John Ringwood) once that a road used to go straight up past that barn, and that's where the old roadway used to be, heading easterly.

Nobody knows who the old man is, but everything about his ghostly activities has now been forgotten in history. The man on his bike has been seen quite a few times going down the hill. And he looks so real, that it is often remarked that he has often tipped his hat in recognition as well, that's quite weird. It is how this short story goes.

ALL SAINTS CHURCH

BRIAN JONES

The Church hall at All Saints, Rhys Street, Trealaw (near Tonypandy), Rhondda is a corrugated iron structure with a hundred years of history behind it. We introduce to you a strange entity residing at the Church hall.

Archaeology Cymru used to hold it's Rhondda classes there, and that is where we have met Brian, who is still a member that lives a few streets away. In talking about ghosts at the meeting we hold now at Pentre, Brian started recollecting about a feeling he used to have at the hall. This next story is delivered to you in the first person; it is a first-hand account.

At the back end of the hall is where we used to do our talks, the front end is where the stage is and on each side is a room. On the right-hand side is an ante-room and on the left, a kitchen. One of the tasks that I had when I was a child; because my mother was the caretaker, was to go down and lock up every evening. Part of the process of locking up was to make sure everything is off, and the heating is off. I never liked running down to that hall or being in that hall in the dark. You had to do this in the dark at night because the lights were switched off at the back. You had to turn these out; then you had to come down to the front of the hall into the kitchen and go out through the kitchen. I never liked it when I was down there; there was a feeling!

I was talking there one night, the Vicar said to me, "do you know one thing about the church hall Brian?"
Brian replied, "what's that?"

Vicar "There is something in that anti-room on the other side!"
Brian "what do you mean by that?"

Vicar "I don't like being in this hall alone there is something there."

Brian "How long have you had that feeling?"

Vicar "since I started here in the parish."

Brian "maybe the feeling that you've had there have been passed from the feelings that I had when I was younger", he looked at me and said, "well what happened with you?"

Brian, "Exactly how I felt", and another person in the group said, "I've had that as well, I've never said that to anybody. What exactly do you think it is?"

Brian, "I don't know; we think it is malign!"

The Vicar that told me this (not the current Vicar Peter), but which Vicar I can't remember, there have been so many vicars.

That was it as far as this story goes, but since that day a few people have said about it occasionally. They felt that there was something there, malign. The presence, its there now. The hall is still the same. It's apparent that the malign entity still resides in the church hall.

I was talking to someone a couple of months ago, they said, "I don't like being in this hall alone". I asked the lady, "why do you say that?" She gave me the same story, but I said the whole place had been rebuilt with a new floor, new walls and a new roof; it wasn't all done at the same time!"

"It doesn't make any difference", she said, "there is something there!" Everybody has just accepted the feeling. The people who have sensed the feeling still think there is something there, and they have got the same feelings about it, that some people have there and they talk about it, some don't talk about it.

THE CHURCH GHOST

MANDIE McCOURT

Often, do we regret to record those stories from our loved ones and when we want to recall them, it is too late, our loved ones have passed on; never again to fill in those missing details, and become those ghosts that this book describes. One such case that epitomizes the above sentiment is the following short story.

Mandie McCourt recalls the ghost seen inside Marcross church, a story from a first-hand account thanks to her mum. Mum was in the church at Marcross, Vale of Glamorgan (West of Llantwit Major) praying. Mum was alone.

When mum was in the process of her prays, focussed in her mind; looking at the back of the pew in front of her, she felt a presence. Mum looked up, and she saw a person stood in front of her. It was a ghostly figure. There is an eerie atmosphere in the church. Alas, my mum is no longer with us, and we were unable to add more to the story.

Its own published ghost story haunts the church at Marcross, once told about a ghost that frequented the yard, hovering above a particular grave. As for explaining Mandie's Mum's spirit, I guess with this story we will never know the detail of what exactly was seen that day, but look up the ghost of Marcross church graveyard, and you shall be enlightened.

THE CHURCH IMAGE

MANDIE McCOURT

My dad (John Ringwood) and husband (Dyfrig McCourt) had just taken me to lunch, and we decided to stop at the church at Llantrithyd, east of Cowbridge, Vale of Glamorgan, on the way back from the A48 heading for Marcross. We went into the churchyard at Llantrithyd; we walked around.

Dad was stood by the yew tree adjacent to the porch, I took a photo through the end window on the left (south side of the church) and then looked through. I remarked to dad that I would freak out if someone looks back at me from the church window.

When we went home, I looked upon the computer, with horror, I saw a face looking back at me through the window, how ironic, after making that joke at the church. With my friends, we viewed the photograph; we saw that there were shadowy forms behind the main image, that I first saw looking back at me.

The image could portray one of the members of the Basset family in the late 1500s that lived at Llantrithyd Place; which is alongside the church. It was once said, that a male member of the Basset family married a woman from Marcross. I may have a link with the lady he married, as my family originates from the Marcross area.

Looking into Llantrithyd Church towards the pulpit. Can you make out the figures? Taken by Mandie McCourt

THE GHOST OF GLADSTONE VILLA

ANDREW DEXTER

A true ghost story that happened to me and my family many years ago.

My family and I lived in a large property known as Gladstone Villa in the former mining town of Bargoed, in the Caerphilly County Borough, near Cardiff. In that property, there were my maternal grandparents William George Higgs; known fondly as Bill to his family and friends, and his wife Rita. My parents Douglas and Karen Dexter they were newly married, we simply experienced things that were beyond rational explanation and imagination. Simply the happenings defied the norm; if there is a norm, there really were footsteps, minor poltergeist activity, actual sightings (though sightings were very rare my mother said).

It all started off very quietly at teatime; the noise was in the attic. The family heard a noise one day when I was a baby, soon after I was born. They may have been thinking they had a 'break-in', it was in the attic, that they felt people sounded as if they were jumping on the landing from the attic. When they went upstairs, they found nothing there, excepting that the hatch door was open now. Whatever it was my family felt that it now occupied itself with the main bedroom, incidentally my grandparent's bedroom.

All sorts of things started to occur. I was a baby at the time; I was too young to remember when it started or any of the early events. My mother said, "all sorts of things that were going on this one day", my mum checked the cot and discovered that the pillow was torn right in half. My mum's friend said that when I was a baby, they had to take me from the bedroom because of what was going on there. As I got older, I experienced it all for myself; I heard the footsteps that were going on most evenings. When actually it would happen during the day sometimes, also, when I was watching television downstairs, but mainly the activity would be in the evening.

This one day I put the television on, and to listen to it more clearly, I was about to put it up, when my grandfather would say, "that the sound is by there", and now we could pinpoint exactly where it was. There was one evening, "this is true!" I was in the bedroom haunted bedroom. I was now on the bed facing the window out to the street light that was on. It was quiet, and suddenly I felt something jumped on the bed, I didn't look straight away because I was scared. When I did eventually look, there was nothing there, it felt like an animal. I went downstairs to see my family to tell them what it was, and they all went up to my bedroom, and they found the claw marks on the bed, "that is true". I found out at some point that my grandfather kept a dog, a black Labrador, called Toby, he died before I was born there, this fact explains the claw marks!

There was one day that my grandmother, got my grandfather out of bed, she said to him "get up", and she said that the door that had the boiler was kept in flung wide open. She didn't look to see what it was; she left the room in a bit of a hurry, so she never found out what that was.

Another family friend Mr Fred Davies that my grandfather used to work with him in the pit, down the mines, and he would visit most evenings. And I remember one particular day it was very quiet, I think Mr Davies came to see us. I was sat by the fireside, always sat by the fireplace; I was playing by the sideboard as children do. Suddenly there was a loud bang; it was so loud that Fred ducked his head. And he later said, when it was quiet, the noise was so loud you thought it was gonna come through! When it was quiet, we all one by one now, went upstairs, my grandfather was first, and I would always be last, when we got to the bedroom there was nothing to account for that noise, nothing.

I remember poltergeist activity, the light going on and off, cables being pulled, and the television going off and then on. At one point my grandfather claimed, he was in the bedroom one day, laying on the bed he couldn't move, he was paralyzed and couldn't shout out to call for help to help him. He heard the floorboards creaking, and I think he said he saw something if I remember rightly, he couldn't move.

At one point my mother and my grandfather Bill could hear a baby crying, at the time I didn't take much notice I didn't hear this in all the years I lived there, I didn't even see it. They contacted another family friend Mrs Ivy France (she died in 2002). Ivy came to visit, she didn't believe my grandmother after being told, that the Gladstone Villa was haunted. I can still remember Ivy coming to investigate this, and going up to the bedroom to see what was going on, Ivy said it was vibrations from the traffic outside causing it. Ivy's opinion seemed to change when she experienced it for her self, and it was Ivy's decision to get the medium involved, the press was mentioned, but my grandmother she felt that she would be ridiculed because of the reports of the activity. So when the local medium was called, his name may have been John Matthews. He questioned the family when he finally began to perform he challenged the spirit, he knocked on the ceiling, and a couple of times, sure enough, the spirit knocked back at his room. And at some point, the medium went into a trance to make timely contact with the spirit, but he failed to get a name. That's when he came around out of the trance, he said this is blatantly obvious that there was a presence there. The medium said this spirit is an earthbound spirit.

Then there was the priest who came as well, and said some prayers and blessed the house. It was quiet for a few short months after that. But a spirit came back; it did return and with a vengeance.

There was one evening where my grandmother was reading a book on the settee, with my grandfather Bill and my mother. I was watching television when my mother just so happened to turn towards my grandmother reading the book, and she saw the full figure of a monk standing behind the sofa by the doorway. I didn't see it, the rest of us didn't take any notice, we were watching television, and my grandmother reading a book. My mother later described the monk, as in full monk's typical habit, with a hood over his head. She didn't see the face, she just looked at the figure for one minute, and it was gone. Yet I too had my own experience with the monk; I heard monks chant in the bathroom. We were going to the bathroom where my grandfather said to me "I can't open the door", he said, "he is behind there", you couldn't open the door. I could hear the Gregorian chant.

It got so bad we slept downstairs with the lights on. Really we were that scared; we had it for so long, my grandmother Rita gave a name to it, called 'Johnny', my grandfather would mock the spirit and would shout, "Johnny O", of course, nothing would happen.

We moved in the summer of 1978, two local businessmen bought the property, and they moved in. The property became the Redz Parc Hotel. When I had my 40th birthday there in 2009, the staff told me they heard noises; they would occasionally see things, and hear things, and footsteps.

I did some research into the history of the area. The property is located in Cardiff Road, Bargoed, and directly opposite there is a pub called the RAFA club, and this is one of the oldest buildings Bargoed, dating back to the 1600s. And there is a priests hole there; this is where a priest used to hide; apparently, I was told. That explains the monk that my mother saw.

I also discovered that Gladstone Villa was named after the prime minister William Gladstone. The Kimmiett family lived there in 1924, a Michael and his wife Evelyn (the lady had died by 1970) and their baby son Elvin. Elvin Rowland (there is a notice about him in the Western mail in an issue of 1924) was only four months old when he died there. That does explain the baby crying that my mother and my grandfather had heard. What I've said here is the truth, really it is the truth, I wouldn't lie, as I've nothing to gain by that, I challenge anyone to check out this for those who don't believe, I can assure you that your belief system will be challenged.

THE LLANMAES TRAMP

DESMOND JOHNSON

The Tramp of Llanmaes is a short story based in the small but picturesque village of Llanmaes, north of Llantwit Major, Vale of Glamorgan; it may have occurred sometime in the late 1940's - early 1950's. The story was first told to Desmond Johnson by his dad Bill (William Johnson) who passed away in 1974. The pub in question is probably the very same pub, still fondly frequented at Llanmaes known as the 'The Blacksmiths Arms'.

My dad used to go to one of the pubs in Llanmaes, and he walked out with this bloke; he was a tramp around here. There was a lot of tramps around here in those days. When my dad went into the pub one day, he said to those inside, "I walked out with old George", they said, "you couldn't have done he died a fortnight ago". My dad then went into further detail to those at the pub; he just said, "I walked around with him, walked up to the road tonight with him to the pub".

Imagine the shock on Bill's face as he discovered that the person who he had just been speaking with, had passed away two weeks earlier! Walking back and forth to Llanmaes and Llantwit Major would have passed Bill along with the place of the Llantwit Major gibbet (believed to be close to the modern junction at the traffic lights at the B4265 and Llanmaes Road) at the once apt sounding Gallows Way, now Llanmaes Road. This road is a haunted route where strange noises are to be heard, and the ghost of George had joined those restless spirits of the many victims of the countless judges, who had been hanged centuries earlier for crimes such as stealing a loaf of bread.

THE
BLACK LAKE

STEPHEN INKPEN

For this story, I have taken several pieces of folklore and weaved them into a story; they all relate to the lake and have also been passed along by word of mouth over the years. The name of the ghost (Carw-Forganu) was told to me by an elderly lady who lived in Rhiwgarn Farm when I was very young, all I know is that she was born there and her family had farmed the Black Mountain for generations, I was about 5 years old when she told me this story, so it was around 1980. (I think they are the Evans family?)

The Wizard of the Black Mountain

Long before the modern mapmakers changed its name to 'Mynydd Y Glyn' the people of Trebanog called their mountain 'Mynydd Ddu' (the Black Mountain). At the top of this mountain is the Black Lake and near here in ages past, before the Romans and Saxons and Vikings, stood the original village of Trebanog. In this village, there lived a powerful wizard (probably a Druid!) who was called Carw-Forganu. It was Carw-Forganu who was responsible for protecting the people from the evil spirits of the lake.

The lake is bottomless and deep, within its black waters live the spirit folk who call to you and entice you into their other-world! Once you hear them call, you walk into the lake and never return to the land of the living.

Today there is a thick silt across the top of the lake, and if you are unfamiliar with this spot, you can be tempted to walk across this fair field. But in the centre, there is always water, and if you start across the field you will be pulled under!

Something always stops you though; it's a light voice on the wind that seems to call out,

"Careful or they will get you! Don't go across there!"

and you stop and walk to the top of the hill before looking back, and seeing for the first time the sparkle of dark water in the centre of the 'field'.

It was said by the people of Old Trebanog that the voice you hear is that of Carw-Forganu, whose spirit still guards the people of Trebanog from the folk beneath the Black Lake. And early in the morning and just as the sunsets, you can sometimes see Carw-Forganu standing at the lake edge, warning the spirit folk within the deep black water that he is still here and still on guard!

The Black Lake, Trebanog by Stephen Inkpen

THE GIRL
AT THE STILE

MANDIE McCOURT

This is a story of when my Nan; Mary Ringwood, saw a ghost.

My Nan was walking down the road from the Horseshoe Public inn, Marcross; west of Llantwit Major, towards the church (and the coast). This route is picturesque; it is along a tarmac road which is surrounded by countryside with a stream on the west side. After a short while, my Nan came around the corner towards the old village church, where on the left-hand side (east) there was an old footpath stile.

At the stile, there was a figure of a young girl, being stood still there at the side of the road, that's the ghost. And it wasn't just my Nan who had seen the girl, but she had with her a friend. These are not the only two people who have seen the ghost, but others were walking down to the church are reported to have seen the ghost also quite a few times in the past.

The ghost is not seen of the young girl much now, in-fact no one has reported of that recently. There is not any back story attached either to these women. Just a young girl stood by the stile, so no one knows the history of the story to why she haunts the locality.

Is the girl waiting for someone, a lost lover, is she requiring to be asked a question from a passerby, just as the 'Elizabethan' ghost of the churchyard at Marcross is waiting? The waiting 'Elizabethan' ghost, was soon asked a question. This mystery was solved.

A Prelude to More Stories

The Llanthony Image a story by Karl-James Langford and Michelle Harrhy. We visited Llanthony and a photograph was taken, but in developing this photograph, something amazing was revealed.

We will visit the 'voice' at Ewenny Priory revealed to us after an all night haunted evening. Then we shall turn to more ghosts from Merthyr Mawr, as well as the latest apparitions from Blaen-y-Cwm, with a further story from Marcross of the Girl in the Pub by Kita McCourt in the next book also.

We would so be delighted to hear from you if you can add to our next publication, part two of our ghosts series; Ghosts of South Wales.

Llanthony Abbey, notice the oddity with the image, by Michelle Harrhy

WORD MEANING

Adam De Frankton
the Norman knight that killed King Llewelyn the Last on the 11th December 1282

Banog Girl
A fond title given to women of the village of Trebanog. Banog girls however, should not be made to be fools, they will exact their revenge.

Cymry
It's meaning in the Cymraeg language, refers to the people and the land as one entity.

Dissolution of the Monasteries
An event orchestrated by King Henry VIII (1491 - 1547 CE, his reign started in 1509) in his reign between 1536 until his death.

Into the Gods
Meaning, to be above you. More often used to refer to the attic or top floor of a building.

Iron Age Bank and Ditched Enclosure
Some Archaeologists use this recently coined term to refer to Iron Age hill-forts. Hill-forts were neither defensive in many cases, and certainly didn't have a military purpose, the sites therefore have 'banks and ditches', also they are an 'enclosed' space in the Iron Age, hence the term!

Mackerel Cloud

This term refer to clouds displaying an undulating, rippling pattern, similar in appearance to scales on a fish.

Naily Boots

Simply termed to refer to hob nail boots.

Norman

Invading people of the British Isles that originated from Normandy in France, that have Viking origins.

Shuck

A large menacing Black dog seen prowling throughout the county lanes.

Sion Celwydd

The Cistercian monk that was a brother at the Monknash religious establishment in around the 1300s ce. Sion's story is rarely told, one however that is used as a backdrop for the 'Ghost Experience Cymru' walks.

Stile

A single vertical stone used for pedestrians to cross fields

INDEX